GREENTOWN SCHOOL

GRAPHIC DINOSAURS

PACHYCEPHALOSAURUS

THE THICK-HEADED LIZARD

ILLUSTRATED BY TERRY RILEY,
GARY JEFFREY, JAMIE WEST

PowerKiDS
press™

New York

Published in 2012 by The Rosen Publishing Group, Inc.
29 East 21st Street, New York, NY 10010

Designed and produced by
David West Books

Designed and written by Rob Shone

Photographic credits: 5t, Gary Müller; 5bl, Magnus Kjaergaard; 5br, USGS; 30l, Ballista; 30r, Anky-man.

Library of Congress Cataloging-in-Publication Data
Shone, Rob.
Pachycephalosaurus : the thick headed lizard / by Rob Shone.
p. cm. — (Graphic dinosaurs)
Includes index.
ISBN 978-1-4488-5252-9 (library binding) — ISBN 978-1-4488-5253-6 (pbk.) — ISBN 978-1-4488-5254-3 (6-pack)
1. Pachycephalosaurus—Juvenile literature. I. Title.
QE862.O65S56 2012
567.914—dc22

2010050992

Manufactured in China

CPSIA Compliance Information: Batch #DS1102PK:
For Further Information contact Rosen Publishing, New York, New York at 1-800-237-9932

CONTENTS

WHAT IS A PACHYCEPHALOSAURUS?

PACHYCEPHALOSAURUS MEANS "THICK-HEADED LIZARD."

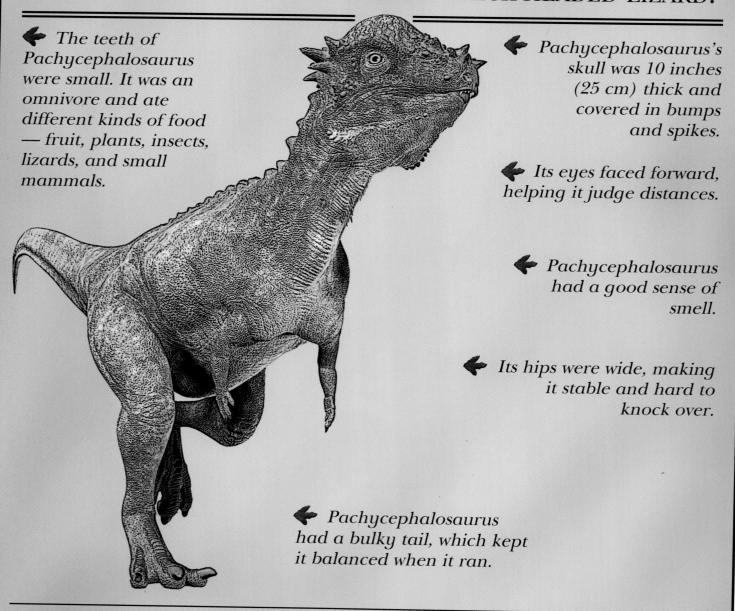

The teeth of Pachycephalosaurus were small. It was an omnivore and ate different kinds of food — fruit, plants, insects, lizards, and small mammals.

Pachycephalosaurus's skull was 10 inches (25 cm) thick and covered in bumps and spikes.

Its eyes faced forward, helping it judge distances.

Pachycephalosaurus had a good sense of smell.

Its hips were wide, making it stable and hard to knock over.

Pachycephalosaurus had a bulky tail, which kept it balanced when it ran.

PACHYCEPHALOSAURUS WAS A DINOSAUR THAT LIVED AROUND 76 MILLION TO 65 MILLION YEARS AGO, DURING THE **CRETACEOUS PERIOD**. **FOSSILS** OF ITS SKELETON HAVE BEEN FOUND IN NORTH AMERICA.

An adult Pachycephalosaurus measured up to 16 feet (5 m) long stood 5 feet (1.5 m) high at the shoulder and weighed up to 1,100 pounds (500 kg).

CRETACEOUS CREATURES

Pachycephalosaurus lived at the end of the Cretaceous period and was one of the last dinosaurs to have existed. It probably lived in small herds, **browsing** on tender leaves and fruit, and sometimes eating insects and lizards.

A raccoon raids a fruit tree (left). Like Pachycephalosauruses, raccoons are omnivores and will eat many different kinds of food.

FAMILY MEMBERS

Two smaller boneheads, Dracorex and Stygimoloch, lived alongside Pachycephalosaurus. Stygimoloch had only a small head dome, while Dracorex did not have a dome at all. Some scientists think these dinosaurs were either females or young Pachycephalosauruses that had not yet grown a full-size dome.

BONE-DOMED DINOSAURS

Ever since the first Pachycephalosaurus skull was found, scientists have wondered why the skulls were so thick. They may have been used to head-butt each other, or to give a rival a painful blow to the side. They may also have been used to fight off dangerous enemies.

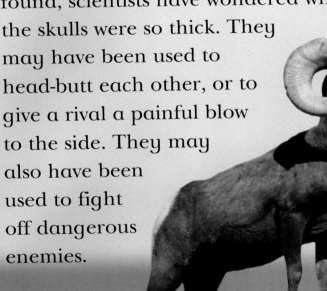

A North American bighorn sheep (left). In the early fall male bighorns fight by head-butting each other (below) to see which one is the stronger. Scientists think that Pachycephalosauruses and other boneheads may have fought in the same way.

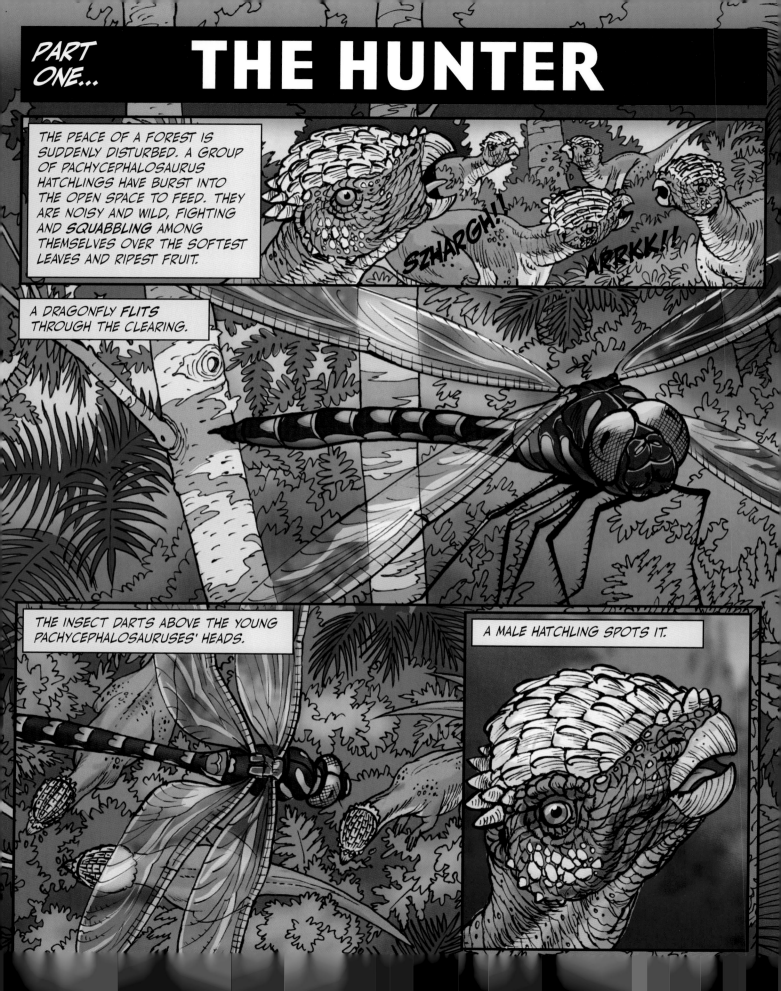

PART ONE

THE HUNTER

THE PEACE OF A FOREST IS SUDDENLY DISTURBED. A GROUP OF PACHYCEPHALOSAURUS HATCHLINGS HAVE BURST INTO THE OPEN SPACE TO FEED. THEY ARE NOISY AND WILD, FIGHTING AND **SQUABBLING** AMONG THEMSELVES OVER THE SOFTEST LEAVES AND RIPEST FRUIT.

SZHARGH!!

ARRKK!!

A DRAGONFLY **FLITS** THROUGH THE CLEARING.

THE INSECT DARTS ABOVE THE YOUNG PACHYCEPHALOSAURUSES' HEADS.

A MALE HATCHLING SPOTS IT.

HE CHASES IT. HE IS HOPING TO CATCH IT AND ENJOY A CRUNCHY SNACK.

PACHYCEPHALOSAURUSES ARE OMNIVORES. THEY EAT FRUIT AND LEAVES AS WELL AS SMALL LIZARDS AND INSECTS.

A TROODON HAS BEEN WATCHING THE LIVELY YOUNG DINOSAURS FROM THE SHADOWS. SHE IS A MEAT EATER, AND THE HATCHLINGS DO NOT LOOK AS IF THEY WILL TEST HER HUNTING SKILLS TOO GREATLY.

A LONE HATCHLING WILL BE EASY PREY. SHE FOLLOWS AS HE RUNS DEEPER INTO THE FOREST.

IN JUST A FEW STRIDES THE TROODON IS CLOSE ENOUGH TO CATCH THE LITTLE DINOSAUR.

THE TROODON PAUSES. SHE HEARS A NOISE COMING FROM THE FERNS.

THREE ANGRY LEPTOCERATOPSES CRASH THROUGH THE **UNDERGROWTH**. THE PLANT EATERS ARE FIGHTING OVER TERRITORY AND DO NOT NOTICE THE TROODON OR THE HATCHLING.

ARRKK!!

ARRKK!!

THE PACHYCEPHALOSAURUS RUNS AWAY BEFORE IT IS TRAMPLED.

THE TROODON IS ALONE. SHE HAS LOST HER MEAL. SHE KNOWS THE REST OF THE HERD ARE NOT FAR AWAY AND TURNS TO FIND THEM.

THEN SHE SEES THE DRAGONFLY...

...WITH THE HATCHLING RUNNING AFTER IT.

SHE FOLLOWS THEM.

NOTHING CAN SAVE THE HATCHLING THIS TIME. THE TROODON HAS HIM TRAPPED.

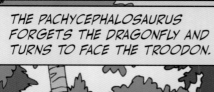

THE PACHYCEPHALOSAURUS FORGETS THE DRAGONFLY AND TURNS TO FACE THE TROODON.

THE TROODON IS SURPRISED. HER VICTIMS USUALLY TRY TO ESCAPE. SHE IS EVEN MORE SURPRISED WHEN THE LITTLE HATCHLING LOWERS HIS HEAD, ALL SET TO ATTACK.

THE MEAT EATER JUMPS BACK AS THE THICKHEAD RUNS AT HER. SHE LOOKS UP. SHE DOES NOT HAVE TO FIND THE REST OF THE HERD. THEY HAVE FOUND HER. THEY ALL HAVE THEIR HEADS LOWERED, READY TO CHARGE.

THE TROODON HAS HAD ENOUGH AND RUNS, LEAVING THE BAD-TEMPERED HATCHLINGS TO FIGHT EACH OTHER.

SZAARRGHH!!

THE DRAGONFLY RETURNS, DARTING ABOVE THE HEADS OF THE QUARRELING HERD. THE HATCHLING SPOTS IT...

...AND CHASES IT.

PART TWO... SWAMP LIFE

IT IS THE RAINY SEASON. A PAIR OF QUETZALCOATLUSES ARE FLYING SOUTH IN SEARCH OF DRIER WEATHER. BENEATH THEM LIES A FLOODED LANDSCAPE OF LAKES AND CREEKS...

...SWAMPS AND MARSHES. A FAMILY OF DRACOREXES ARE FEEDING ON THE WETLAND'S LUSH VEGETATION.

THEY ARE RELATED TO THE PACHYCEPHALOSAURUSES, BUT INSTEAD OF A DOMED HEAD THEY HAVE LARGE SPIKES FOR PROTECTION.

THE DRACOREXES QUICKLY DISAPPEAR INTO THE FLOODED FOREST WHEN THEY SEE THEIR LARGER COUSINS ARRIVE.

THE DRAGONFLY CHASER IS ONE YEAR OLD BUT IS NOT YET FULL-GROWN.

THE HERD BEGINS TO FEED ON TASTY FRUIT AND LEAVES...

...AND TENDER, JUICY WATER PLANTS.

WHILE THE WINGED REPTILES CAN ESCAPE THE WET SEASON, MOST OTHER ANIMALS HAVE TO STAY. BUT WITH THE RAIN COMES A **BOUNTY** OF FOOD. BIRDS, MAMMALS, DINOSAURS, AND REPTILES ALL ENJOY THE HARVEST.

NONE OF THE ANIMALS NOTICES THE DARK SHAPE MOVING BENEATH THE WATER.

THE PACHYCEPHALOSAURUSES DO SEE A PAIR OF CHIROSTENOTES ON THE OPPOSITE BANK. THEY USE THEIR TOOTHLESS BEAKS TO HUNT FOR INSECTS AND SMALL REPTILES.

THEY ARE NOT A THREAT, BUT THE THICKHEADS SCREAM OUT WARNING CRIES TO SCARE THEM AWAY.

ARRHHHKR!!

THE CHIROSTENOTES TURN AND RUN. BUT IT IS NOT THE THICKHEADS THAT HAVE MADE THEM LEAVE.

NOR IS IT THE DARK SHAPE BENEATH THE WATER MOVING TOWARD THE BANK.

SOMETHING IS COMING.

A HERD OF PANICKING ANATOTITANS CHARGE OUT OF THE UNDERGROWTH STRAIGHT AT THE PACHYCEPHALOSAURUSES.

CHASING THE PLANT EATERS IS A GIGANTIC TYRANNOSAURUS.

ROUAGHHH!!!

THE HUGE MEAT EATER AND TERRIFIED ANATOTITANS CRASH AND SPLASH THROUGH THE SWAMP.

THE DRAGONFLY CHASER HAS BEEN CUT OFF FROM THE HERD AND IS IN THE PATH OF THE STAMPEDING DINOSAURS. HE WADES THROUGH THE MUDDY WATER AS FAST AS HE CAN.

HE IS TOO SLOW. THE TYRANNOSAURUS SEES HIM.

THE DARK SHAPE SUDDENLY *ERUPTS* FROM THE WATER. IT IS A *DEINOSUCHUS.* THE ENORMOUS ALLIGATOR GRABS THE TYRANNOSAURUS IN ITS POWERFUL JAWS.

GRAGHHH!!

THE TYRANNOSAURUS MANAGES TO TWIST FREE AND BITE THE REPTILE BACK.

18

THE LITTLE PACHYCEPHALOSAURUS DOES NOT STOP TO WATCH THE TWO GIANTS FIGHTING.

ON EITHER SIDE OF HIM ANATOTITANS GALLOP PAST.

EVENTUALLY THE SWAMP BECOMES CALM AGAIN AND THE DRAGONFLY CHASER STOPS RUNNING. HE CAN SEE THE REST OF THE HERD AND GOES TO JOIN THEM.

MEANWHILE, AS THE TYRANNOSAURUS LIMPS PAINFULLY AWAY, THE DEINOSUCHUS SLIPS BACK INTO THE WATER LEAVING BEHIND A TRAIL OF BLOOD FROM ITS WOUNDS.

PART THREE

T. REX ATTACK

A TREE SHATTERS, SMASHED INTO A THOUSAND SPLINTERS BY A BONY BALL THE SIZE OF A TRASH CAN.

KERRACKK!!!

A FEMALE EUOPLOCEPHALUS HAS SWISHED HER TAIL CLUB AT HER ATTACKERS AND MISSED. SHE TURNS TO PROTECT HER CALF AND PREPARES TO SWING HER TAIL AGAIN.

HER ATTACKERS ARE THREE YOUNG TYRANNOSAURUSES. THEY ARE NOT BIG ENOUGH TO HARM THE MOTHER EUOPLOCEPHALUS, BUT THEY ARE BIG ENOUGH TO KILL THE CALF.

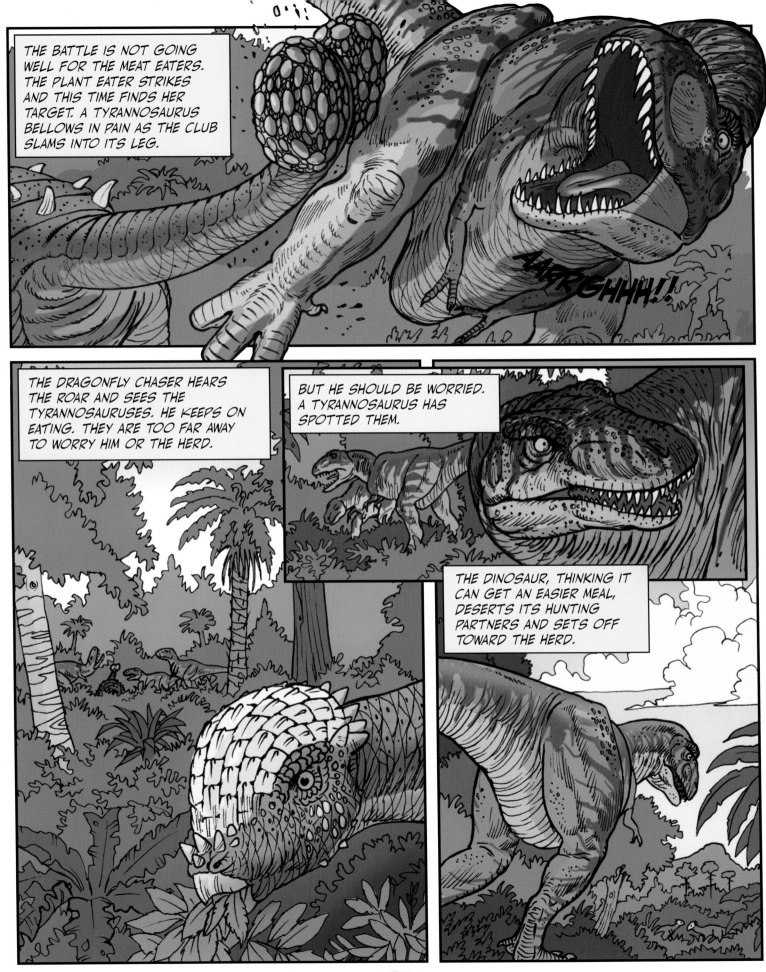

THE BATTLE IS NOT GOING WELL FOR THE MEAT EATERS. THE PLANT EATER STRIKES AND THIS TIME FINDS HER TARGET. A TYRANNOSAURUS BELLOWS IN PAIN AS THE CLUB SLAMS INTO ITS LEG.

AARRGHHH!!

THE DRAGONFLY CHASER HEARS THE ROAR AND SEES THE TYRANNOSAURUSES. HE KEEPS ON EATING. THEY ARE TOO FAR AWAY TO WORRY HIM OR THE HERD.

BUT HE SHOULD BE WORRIED. A TYRANNOSAURUS HAS SPOTTED THEM.

THE DINOSAUR, THINKING IT CAN GET AN EASIER MEAL, DESERTS ITS HUNTING PARTNERS AND SETS OFF TOWARD THE HERD.

A SUDDEN PAIN IN ITS LEG STOPS THE TYRANNOSAURUS FROM KILLING THE THICKHEAD. THE DRAGONFLY CHASER HAS RAMMED IT.

ANOTHER DOMED HEAD CRASHES INTO THE MEAT EATER'S RIBS. THE TYRANNOSAURUS YELLS OUT IN RAGE, AND IS HIT AGAIN, THIS TIME IN THE LEFT LEG.

SNARGHH!!

THE PACHYCEPHALOSAURUSES DART QUICKLY IN AND OUT, LEAVING THE ANGRY TYRANNOSAURUS SNAPPING AT THIN AIR. ITS SIDE, THIGH, AND TAIL ARE ALL POUNDED TO A PULP.

ROUARRR!!

LATER, THE TWO YOUNG TYRANNOSAURUSES WANDER PAST THEIR PARTNER. THEY HAVE NOT BEEN SUCCESSFUL EITHER, AND ONE IS LIMPING BADLY. AT LEAST THEY ARE ON THEIR FEET. THE THIRD TYRANNOSAURUS IS ON ITS SIDE AND HAS NOT MOVED SINCE THE THICKHEADS LEFT. IT WILL LEAVE THE VIOLENT DINOSAURS ALONE FROM NOW ON IF IT EVER RECOVERS.

PART FOUR...
THE LEADER
A GROUP OF ORNITHOMIMUSES DASHES HEADLONG THROUGH THE FOREST, DESPERATELY TRYING TO ESCAPE.
THEY ARE RUNNING NOT FROM A HUNGRY TYRANNOSAURUS, BUT FROM AN ANGRY PACHYCEPHALOSAURUS.
IT IS THE BREEDING SEASON, AND THE LEADER OF THE THICKHEAD HERD IS EVEN GRUMPIER THAN USUAL. HE WILL CHASE AWAY ANY ANIMAL IN HIS TERRITORY, EVEN ORNITHOMIMUSES.
WAARGHHH!!

HIS RULE IS THREATENED BY YOUNGER MALES. A DISPLAY OF POWER AND STRENGTH IS ENOUGH TO SCARE MOST OF THEM OFF.

A SHARP BUTT TO THE SIDE DRIVES AWAY THE REST...

...EXCEPT FOR ONE. THE DRAGONFLY CHASER HAS BECOME A LARGE AND STRONG ADULT. HE IS READY TO CHALLENGE FOR THE LEADERSHIP.

THE LEADER ROARS
AT THE CHALLENGER,
WHO ROARS BACK
JUST AS LOUDLY.

ROARGHH!!

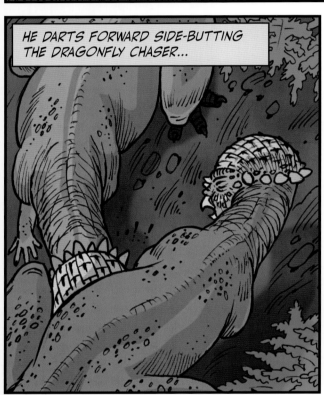

HE DARTS FORWARD SIDE-BUTTING
THE DRAGONFLY CHASER...

...WHO SPINS AROUND
AND BUTTS THE
LEADER IN RETURN.

SIDE-BUTTING AND A SHOW
OF STRENGTH HAVE NOT
WORKED. THERE MUST BE
ANOTHER WAY TO DECIDE THE
WINNER. THE TWO RIVALS
STAND A FEW PACES APART.

WUARGHH!!

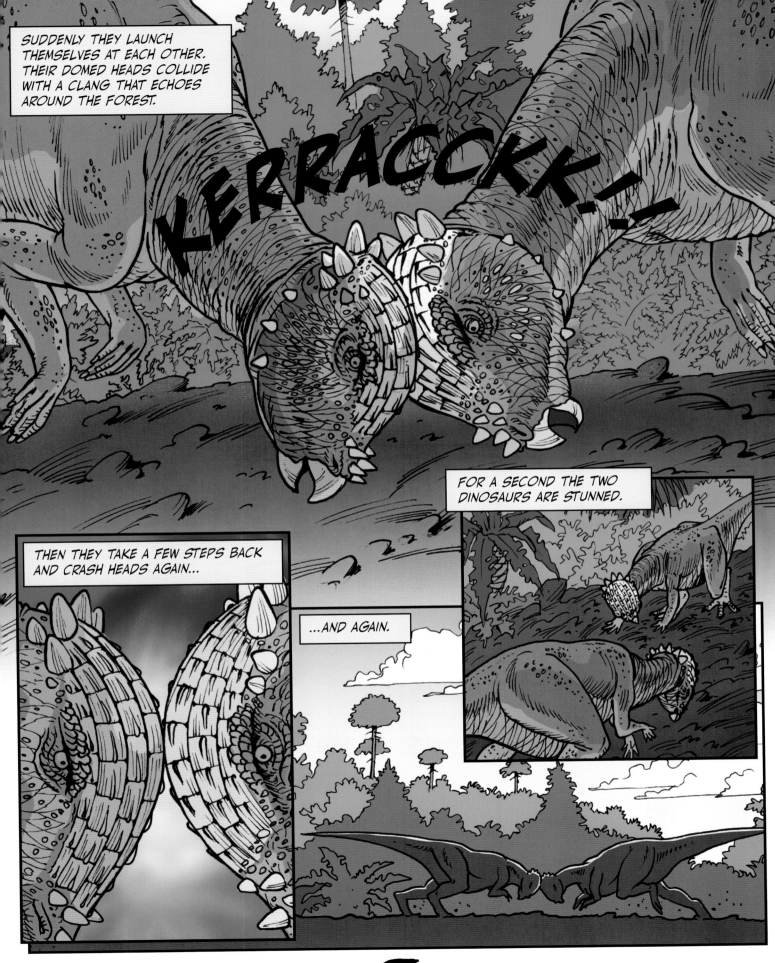

SUDDENLY THEY LAUNCH THEMSELVES AT EACH OTHER. THEIR DOMED HEADS COLLIDE WITH A CLANG THAT ECHOES AROUND THE FOREST.

KERRACCKK!!!

FOR A SECOND THE TWO DINOSAURS ARE STUNNED.

THEN THEY TAKE A FEW STEPS BACK AND CRASH HEADS AGAIN...

...AND AGAIN.

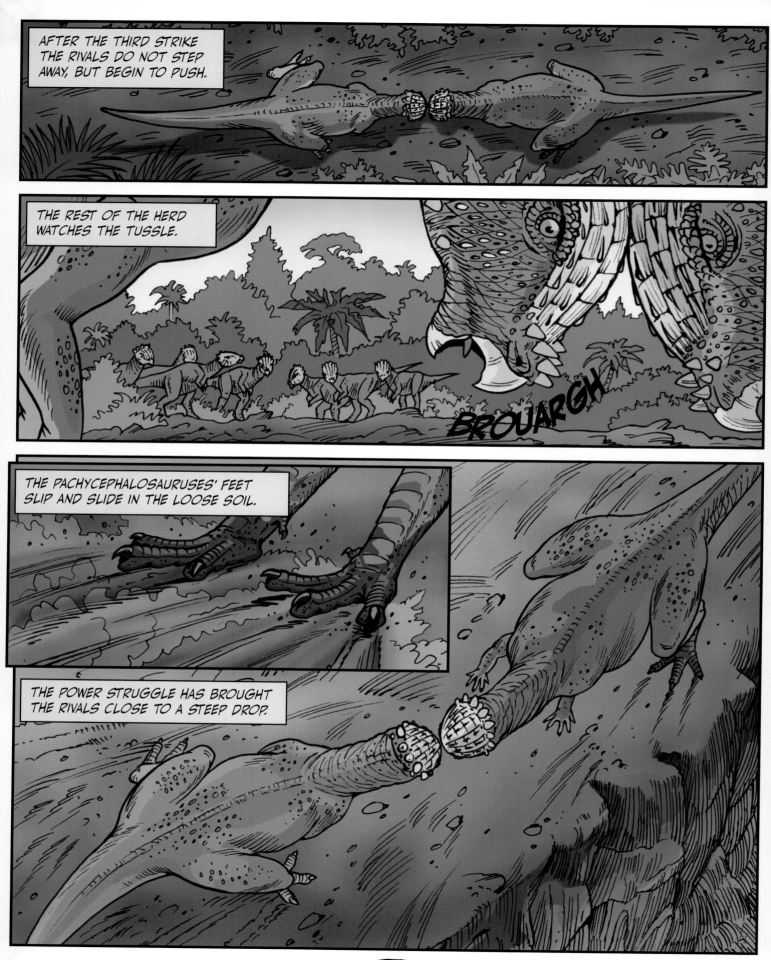

AFTER THE THIRD STRIKE THE RIVALS DO NOT STEP AWAY, BUT BEGIN TO PUSH.

THE REST OF THE HERD WATCHES THE TUSSLE.

BROUARGH

THE PACHYCEPHALOSAURUSES' FEET SLIP AND SLIDE IN THE LOOSE SOIL.

THE POWER STRUGGLE HAS BROUGHT THE RIVALS CLOSE TO A STEEP DROP.

THE DRAGONFLY CHASER GIVES ONE LAST PUSH, AND THE OLD MALE TUMBLES OVER THE EDGE.

WAARRKK!!!

THE OLD LEADER'S RULE IS OVER. HE IS HURT, BUT HE WILL LIVE.

THE DRAGONFLY CHASER ROARS IN TRIUMPH AND PREPARES TO LEAD THE HERD.

FOSSIL EVIDENCE

SCIENTISTS LEARN WHAT DINOSAURS MAY HAVE LOOKED LIKE BY STUDYING THEIR FOSSIL REMAINS. FOSSILS ARE FORMED WHEN THE HARD PARTS OF AN ANIMAL OR PLANT ARE BURIED AND TURN TO ROCK OVER THOUSANDS OF YEARS.

A nearly complete Pachycephalosaurus skull was found at the Hell Creek Formation, Montana, (below), in 1943.

In 1859 fossil hunter Donald Baird found thick pieces of fossilized bone in Montana. At the time scientists thought they were part of the skin armor of a reptile. When the bones were studied again a century later, they were discovered to be part of a Pachycephalosaurus skull. Scientists were amazed at how thick the skull was, up to 10 inches (25 cm) in places. Why would any animal need a skull that thick?

Pachycephalosaurus's head may have been large, but its brain was tiny.

Scientists first thought that the skulls were used in head-butting contests, like the ones some modern-day goats and sheep have. But some scientists argued that the force would have cracked their skulls, broken their necks, and killed them. However, recent studies using computer models have shown that the skulls were more than strong enough to take the strain. Until more fossil evidence is found, no one will know for sure why Pachycephalosaurus's skulls were so thick.

ANIMAL GALLERY

ALL THESE ANIMALS APPEAR IN THE STORY.

Leptoceratops
"Lean-horned face"
Length: 6.5 ft (2 m)
A small plant eater and relative of the gigantic Triceratops.

Troodon
"Wounding tooth"
Length: 8 ft (2.5 m)
This meat-eating dinosaur's brain was large for its size.

Chirostinotes
"Narrow hand"
Length: 9.5 ft (3 m)
A fast-moving meat-eater with very powerful claws.

Dracorex
"Dragon king"
Length: 9.5 ft (3 m)
An omnivore like its larger relative, Pachycephalosaurus.

Ornithomimus
"Bird mimic"
Length: 12 ft (4 m)
A fast-moving omnivore that had a toothless beak.

Euoplocephalus
"Well-armored head"
Length: 20 ft (6 m)
An armored plant eater that had a bony club on the end of its tail.

Quetzalcoatlus
"Bird serpent"
Wingspan: 33 ft (10 m)
A reptile and one of the world's largest flying animals.

Anatotitan
"Giant duck"
Length: 38 ft (11.5 m)
A large duck-billed plant eater that weighed about 3.3 tons (3,000 kg).

Deinosuchus
"Terrible crocodile"
Length: 40 ft (12 m)
A huge alligator with a bite twice as strong as any present-day animal's.

Tyrannosaurus
"Tyrant lizard"
Length: 42.5 ft (13 m)
A huge meat eater that was the top land predator of its day.

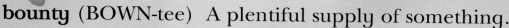

GLOSSARY

bounty (BOWN-tee) A plentiful supply of something.

browsing (BROW-zing) Feeding on high-growing vegetation.

Cretaceous period (krih-TAY-shus PIR-ee-ud) The time between 146 million and 65 million years ago.

erupts (ih-RUPTS) Bursts out suddenly.

flits (FLITS) Moves quickly and suddenly.

fossils (FO-sulz) The remains of living things that have turned to rock.

prey (PRAY) Animals that are hunted for food by another animal.

squabbling (SKWA-beh–ling) Arguing noisily over little things.

undergrowth (UN-der-grohwth) Dense woodland vegetation.

INDEX

Web Sites
Due to the changing nature of Internet links, the Rosen Publishing Group, Inc., has developed an online list of Web sites related to the subject of this book. This site is updated regularly. Please use this link to access the list:
www.powerkidslinks.com/gdino/pach/